This Is My Book / Éste es mi libro

By/por Amanda Hudson

Reading Consultant: Susan Nations, M.Ed.,
author/literacy coach/consultant in literacy development/
Consultora de lectura: Susan Nations, M.Ed.,
autora/tutora de alfabetización/consultora de desarrollo de lectoescritura

WEEKLY READER®
PUBLISHING

Please visit our web site at www.garethstevens.com
For a free catalog describing our list of high-quality books,
call 1-800-542-2595 (USA) or 1-800-387-3178 (Canada).
Our fax: 1-877-542-2596

Library of Congress Cataloging-in-Publication Data

Hudson, Amanda.
     (This is my book. Spanish & English)
     This is my book = Este es mi libro / Amanda Hudson.
       p. cm. — (Our toys = Nuestros juguetes)
     ISBN-10: 0-8368-9258-5   ISBN-13: 978-0-8368-9258-1 (lib. bdg.)
     ISBN-10: 0-8368-9357-3   ISBN-13: 978-0-8368-9357-1 (softcover)
  1. Vocabulary—Juvenile literature. I. Title. II. Title: Este es mi libro.
PE1449.H7418   2009
428.1—dc22   2008014469

This edition first published in 2009 by
Weekly Reader® Books
An Imprint of Gareth Stevens Publishing
1 Reader's Digest Road
Pleasantville, NY 10570-7000 USA

Senior Managing Editor: Lisa M. Herrington
Creative Director: Lisa Donovan
Electronic Production Manager: Paul Bodley, Jr.
Designer: Alexandria Davis
Photographer: Richard Hutchings
Cover Designer: Amelia Favazza, *Studio Montage*
Translation: Tatiana Acosta and Guillermo Gutiérrez

Printed in the United States of America

1 2 3 4 5 6 7 8 9 10 09 08

Note to Educators and Parents

Learning to read is one of the most exciting and challenging things young children do. Among other skills, they are beginning to match the spoken word to print and learn directionality and print conventions.

The books in the *Our Toys* series are designed to support young readers in the earliest stages of literacy. Children will love looking at the full-color photographs while also being challenged to think about words that name objects and how those words fit into a basic sentence structure.

In addition to serving as wonderful picture books in schools, libraries, and homes, this series is specifically intended to be read within instructional small groups. The small group setting enables the teacher or other adult to provide scaffolding that will boost the reader's efforts. Children and adults alike will find these books supportive, engaging, and fun!

—Susan Nations, M.Ed.,
author, literacy coach, and consultant in literacy development

Nota para los maestros y los padres

Aprender a leer es una de las actividades más emocionantes y estimulantes que realizan los niños pequeños. Entre otras destrezas, a esta edad están comenzando a integrar su manejo del lenguaje oral con el lenguaje escrito, y a aprender las convenciones de la letra impresa y la dirección de la lectura.

Los libros de la colección *Nuestros juguetes* están pensados para ayudar a los jóvenes lectores en las primeras etapas del proceso de lectoescritura. A los niños les gustará mirar las fotografías a todo color y pensar en los nombres de los objetos, y en cómo estas palabras encajan en la estructura básica de una oración.

Además de servir como maravillosos libros ilustrados en escuelas, bibliotecas y hogares, los libros de esta colección han sido especialmente concebidos para ser leídos en grupos de lectura guiada. Este contexto permite que un maestro u otro adulto proporcione la orientación necesaria para estimular el esfuerzo de los lectores. ¡Estos libros les resultarán útiles, estimulantes y divertidos a niños y a adultos por igual!

— Susan Nations, M.Ed.,
autora/tutora de alfabetización/consultora de desarrollo de la lectura

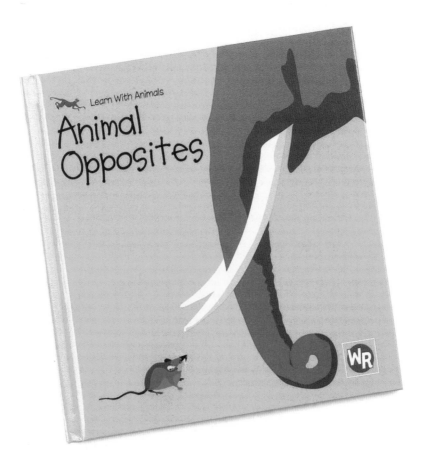

picture book
- - - - - -
libro de dibujos

This is my picture book.
- - - - - - - - - -
Éste es mi libro de dibujos.

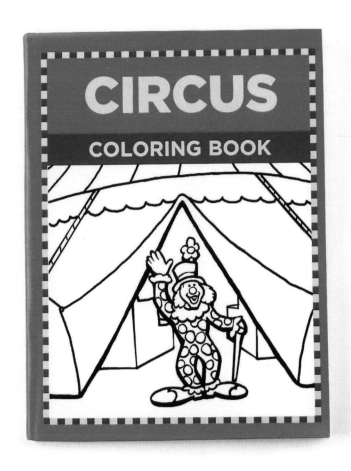

coloring book
- - - - - -
libro de colorear

This is my coloring book.
- - - - - - - - - -
Éste es mi libro de colorear.

BEHOLD, THE CASTLE!

A full moon rises over the hill and lights up everyone once each day. It sheds hundreds of feet to the edge of a rocky cliff. Watchtowers tore above the battlements, where armed guards pace. Torches blaze on the gatehouse, a sort of semi-fortress above a spiked iron gate. Moonlight sparkles on the water slowly encircling the massive moat just outside the castle.

Castles were the showpieces of the Middle Ages (A.D. 500 to A.D. 1500). They were the homes of kings and the lords of life for communities. Within the walls of these mighty fortresses you could mill grains, skin a horse, feast on pig's head, say your prayers in the chapel, pay your taxes, or battle for protection against warring invaders.

The Middle Ages were a time of great power struggles among the kings, barons, and knights who ruled feudal society. Their medieval castles were usually built high on a hill or cliff. That way you could spot your enemies coming — and observe them with clearly armies as they climbed uphill. Without an impressive and impregnable castle, you'd be in danger of losing your estate, your title, your lands — even your head!

STICKS AND STONES

The first European castles were built around A.D. 1066. They bore wooden towers and timber walls were cheap and fast to build and put up quick to catch fire. By the twelfth century, stone was spread and erected fortunable walls, buildings, and towers. Wardens scrabbling shaped the young structure. Heavy building materials were hauled up by simple cranes powered by men trudging in treadmill wheels. It was expensive, time-consuming work. The castle walls, often could be three feet thick and twenty feet high!

A watery moat circled the castle. The most kept the walls supplies with tasty fish and waterfowl. It also helped keep enemy armies from scaling the castle walls. When the drawbridge was down, peasants, tradesmen, knights, pilgrims, peddlers, musicians, and others weary, clattered into the castle under the watchful eyes of the gatehouse guards. But if trouble threatened, the portcullis thundered down. This heavy wood and iron gate with dangerously spiked tips was also dropped to shield, or a would-be's hard castle. The gatecully kept the enemy at the gate.

pop-up book
- - - - - - -
libro desplegable

This is my pop-up book.
- - - - - - - - - -
Éste es mi libro desplegable.

counting book

- - - - - - -

libro para contar

This is my counting book.
- - - - - - - - - -
Éste es mi libro para contar.

story book

libro de cuentos

This is my story book.
— — — — — — — — —
Éste es mi libro de cuentos.

13

ABC book

– – – – – –

abecedario

This is my ABC book.
- - - - - - - - - - -
Éste es mi abecedario.

This is not a book!
– – – – – – –
¡Esto no es un libro!

16